Naturism and Christianity: Are They Compatible?

Karen Gorham

Priest-in-Charge of St Paul's, Maidstone

Dave Leal

Lecturer in Philosophy and Moral Theology,
Regent's Park College, Oxford

GROVE BOOKS LIMITED

RIDLEY HALL RD CAMBRIDGE CB3 9HU

Contents

The Cover Illustration is by Peter Ashton

First Impression July 2000
ISSN 1470-854X
ISBN 1 85174 438 X

1
Introduction

Can Christians be naturists? Might it even be the case that Christians *ought to be* naturists? Our primary purpose in writing this booklet has been to investigate the extent to which naturism is consistent with Christian faith. However, in the course of the investigation we will see reasons why Christians might be more than just tolerant of naturism, but might actually see something of positive value in it. In discussing this subject, we need to see something of the history of the modern naturist movement. We also need to understand a little of the history of Christian attitudes towards the body and nakedness. To do so, it is helpful to reflect upon the theology of nakedness, both in the Bible and in the development of Christian thought, so that we can see why these attitudes developed in the way they did, and how we should respond today. In the light of description, history and theology we seek at the end of the booklet to offer some provisional answers to our initial questions.

If the number of television documentaries about it is anything to judge by, there is considerable interest in the subject of naturism. Or perhaps that is far too naive a view? Documentaries about naturism, and holiday programmes featuring naturist resorts, provide an obvious form of legitimation for the showing of naked bodies. Naked bodies (or the promise of them) may be good for audience statistics. So perhaps it is not the subject of naturism *as such* which is interesting. It is notable that the programmes have tended to be on commercial television! Whatever the truth lying behind the suspicion here, there is something important in its very plausibility.

What makes it plausible is something to do with the conjunction of a medium such as television and human nakedness. Many people who are interested in watching such a documentary will do so just for the sake of seeing naked human bodies. They will not be interested in naturism, or at least not interested in it in some of its more sympathetic forms. Indeed, there is an odd problem in showing a programme about naturism on television. The medium lends itself to the portrayal of nudity as pornographic. It is nudity without a proper context in life, accessible to the viewer at the press of a button. Under such circumstances the body can easily become subject to appraisal as a kind of object. Many naturists would aspire to exactly the opposite viewpoint, seeking to integrate nakedness and the body into the whole of life. One brief self-definition of naturism is as 'a way of living in harmony with nature, characterized by the practice of communal nudity.'[1] It is this understanding of naturism which will most concern us in what follows.

---

1   14th International Naturist Congress, Agde, 1974.

2
Naturism: A Brief History

Today naturism is a growing world-wide movement. In Britain alone the membership of the Central Council of British Naturism (CCBN) has risen by 20 per cent in the last five years and there are an estimated 500,000 naturists and 30,000 members of naturist clubs. In Germany it has been estimated that 19.5% of the population are naturists, though this probably assumes quite a wide definition of 'naturist'! The first official naturist beach in Britain was opened near Hastings in the late 1970s and since then it has been possible to find such beaches all around the British coast where clothing is optional. More and more people are finding the freedom of going without clothes appealing, and there are now about 130 naturist clubs in this country.

Naturism as we know it today had its British origins in the 1920s,[2] though as long ago as 1779 Lord Monboddo, a Scottish judge, advocated naked air bathing. Freidrich Ludwig John was responsible the inclusion of physical education into the German school system in 1811. The reason was to keep Germans fit under French occupation; nude sunbathing formed part of this programme. In 1903 sun and air bathing clinics were established both in Switzerland and in England. In the 1920s naked bathing was authorized by the Government in Denmark. Naturism began with the idealism of a simple, natural lifestyle of healthy living and outdoor recreation at one with nature. The first naturist club was set up in England in 1923.

Organized 'nudism' spread from Europe into Britain during the early 1930s when there was a 'great outdoor' movement including activities such as hiking, cycling and camping. The European stronghold was Germany and development continued until the time of the Nazi domination when Hitler outlawed the nudist movement. Several reasons have been offered for this, one being its association with the terrible poverty suffered between the wars, when large communities took to the woods and literally lived off the land. During the summer months no clothes were worn, thus saving what little clothing people had for the cold weather. Another reason may have been the Nazi desire to split up any gatherings of people, particularly where such groups or gatherings included intellectuals. Though progress in Germany was thus stopped, there was slow growth in Britain, and several clubs were established.

In those pioneer days, small groups gathered on plots of woodland rented from farmers. In some cases, land was purchased and member-owned clubs were established. Many of these exist today. Camping was primitive compared with

---

2   Though the Central Council for British Naturism web site notes the existence of a 'short-lived "Fellowship of the Naked Trust"…in British India with objects and ideals similar to many later clubs' in 1891, it dates the start of formal British activities to 1922.

today's standards and most members were strict vegetarians, with alcohol and tobacco definitely prohibited.

In the immediate post-war years, a new growth pattern emerged. The word 'nudism' was replaced by 'naturism' because it was felt that the former over-emphasized nakedness when, in actual fact, time spent naked is small and de-pendent upon the weather. Naturism was presented to the public as a healthy family recreation—many clubs have more children in their membership than ei-ther men or women. Facilities are both indoor and outdoor. A few clubs are little more than sun-bathing areas, while others have several tennis courts, sun-bath-ing lawns and swimming pools. More than seventy clubs, grouped into eight Regional Associations, form the national body of the CCBN.

Today, many people are at times able to accept nudity as a matter of course. In various countries (though not in England) there are public resorts where normal family life can be led openly and easily by naked people. One such is Cap d'Agde, a resort on the Mediterranean coast in Southern France. This is a holiday area built in the 1970s under the auspices of the French Government. Holiday-makers of all ages go there, and people visiting adjust quickly to the situation and appear to enjoy an exhilarating sense of freedom.

In Britain there are now a growing number of naturist swimming sessions at local swimming pools, and of naturist beaches—both official and unofficial. The attitude of the public to these demonstrates quite well the differences of opinion about naturism and nakedness. There is the example of Studland Bay in Dorset, where the policy of the National Trust and sensitive policing by Dorset Constabu-lary have created one of the finest and safest naturist beaches in the world. On a summer's day, up to five thousand people enjoy peaceful nude recreation. How-ever, because of the difficulty in differentiating between nuisance and nudity, naturism has been banned from other beaches around the country.

Currently the CCBN are promoting the concept of 'nude tolerance'—a cam-paign for greater tolerance of nudity in society, and particularly on Britain's beaches and open spaces. There is ongoing discussion on the subject of decency and offen-siveness, the public and the private, and the need for proper guidelines, codes of conduct and respect.[3]

---

3   In Holland the 'zoning' of beaches is common practice, and Resort Guides indicate the sections of the beach that are used by naturists. There is a policy intended to ensure proper behaviour and contain and control irresponsible activities.

3
The Meanings of Nakedness

The kinds of images which are utilised in that 'soft' pornography market which is the stock in trade of the *middle* shelves (let alone the top shelves!) of our newsagents' shops are only a part of a much fuller realm of symbol and meaning. Nakedness has many associations. The following list is not intended to be exhaustive, but to give some idea of the range of ways in which nakedness can serve as a potent image, conjuring up a variety of different ideas. Some of these are obvious and literal, others are not. But they indicate the capacity of the rich range of meanings of the concept of nakedness. It is worth presenting them here, if only to prevent us leaping too quickly and exclusively to an association of nakedness and the erotic.

- Innocence: the nakedness of the newborn baby as a symbol of innocence. Clothes can be a mask, and their absence a symbol by way of contrast of our capacity (and perhaps our need or desire) to hide our true selves.
- Vulnerability: again, the newborn baby may serve as a powerful image of a need for protection. Clothes can cover and protect against cold and wet, and can be armour against attack. There are biblical examples perhaps indicating dependency in Job 1.21 and Ecclesiastes 5.15, and helplessness in Hosea 2.3.
- Poverty: the incapacity to afford clothing can mean the necessity of going naked. This may carry consequent implications of pity and shame, though here the pity and shame do not focus on the nakedness as much as they do upon the poverty which causes it. We see an association of poverty and nakedness in Job 24.4–10, though here the nakedness appears at least in part to be the result of specific acts of oppression. The association of nakedness and humiliation is emphasized in Amos 2.16.
- Punishment: perhaps connected with humiliation, the stripping of those to be punished may emphasize their degradation and vulnerability in the face of the power of those who inflict punishment. Christians may particularly recall the stripping of Jesus for crucifixion.
- Madness and possession: the story of the demoniac in the Gospel of Mark implies this connection (see Mark 5.15, where the restored demoniac is described as 'clothed and in his right mind.') Compare Calvin's comment: 'Though we are not tormented by the devil, yet he holds us as his slaves, till the Son of God delivers us from his tyranny. Naked, torn and disfigured, we wander about, till he restores us to soundness of mind.'[4]
- Power: Roman emperors once 'showed their unchallenged power by posing

---

4   Quoted in C E B Cranfield, *The Gospel According to Saint Mark* (Cambridge: CUP, 1959) p 180.

in the nude, thereby recapturing the heroic ease and readiness associated with the deathless gods' (though this was subject to change under Christian influence).[5]

- Transparency/openness: we may speak of being 'laid bare' before someone, perhaps involuntarily, and Christians may hold their lives to be lived in a special aspect of transparent nakedness of this sort towards God. Interestingly, a word used in the Septuagint (the Greek translation of the Old Testament) for making bare or uncovering, the Hebrew '*rh*, is *apokalypto*—reveal, disclose—from which we get the word (now a very-long-dead metaphor) apocalypse!

- Sexual connotations: nakedness is associated with sexual arousal or availability, though the teasing promise of nakedness (semi-nakedness) may serve this purpose rather better than actual nakedness![6] This same teasing nakedness reduced to an object may serve to provoke irrelevant erotic associations with market goods through advertising. Actual nakedness as presented pictorially often functions in an importantly different way, presenting the naked person as an object.

None of these need have any special claim to be thought of as *the* meaning of nakedness. In fact, it might be the case that none of them have any necessary part to play in an analysis of nakedness. Even if the sexual connotations of nakedness are most obvious in cultures such as our own, where sexual obsession and sexual display are most marked, there is no reason to imagine that all cultures must experience nakedness that way.

4
Nakedness in Scripture

We have connected most of the accounts of the meaning of nakedness above with biblical references. There is, however, no *direct* discussion of nakedness as such in the Bible, and it is left to us to interpret the meaning of nakedness and its significance from the various contexts in which it is mentioned. A few Old Testament passages may spring readily to mind, such as David dancing before the Ark of the Covenant, after which he is rebuked by Michal: 'How the king of Israel distinguished himself today! He uncovered himself in the eyes of his servants' maids

---

5   Peter Brown, *The Body and Society* (London: Faber and Faber, 1989) p 438.
6   See the remarkable discussion of veiling and the erotic in relation to 1 Corinthians 11.2–16 in Francis Watson, *Agape, Eros, Gender* (Cambridge: CUP, 2000) chapter 2.

as one of the foolish ones shamelessly uncovers himself!' (2 Samuel 6.20). Yet this can hardly be taken as proof of a condemnation of nakedness *per se* in the Bible. One obvious reason for this is that Michal's attitude is rejected by David himself. The author of 2 Samuel interpolates a brief aside (6.23) in such a way as to imply God's judgment on her for this.

More important reasons exist relevant to our purposes, though. What is condemned is not the uncovering, but the demeaning nature of the activity[7]—demeaning, that is, to one of David's royal dignity. What constitutes undignified activity is largely a matter of social convention; it is not David's dignity before God that Michal worries about, but his dignity before the servants' maids. So we are being forced to ask after the social meaning of forms of nakedness. And that may vary, historically and culturally.

In this regard, it is interesting to note the differing areas in which nakedness is mentioned in the context of prophetic action and witness. In 1 Samuel 19.23, 24 we read of Saul prophesying and lying naked all day and night. Perhaps the proverb at the end of v 24 is intended simply to call up an association with 1 Samuel 10.1–13, but it seems to imply that nakedness was something regularly associated with prophecy. In Ezekiel (16.7, 22) nakedness is used as an image provoking explicitly sexual imagery, yet the imagery does not provoke a responding image of rape or violation, but of marriage, of care and of tenderness. The overriding meaning is of a woman lying helplessly stripped bare and vulnerable. This reliance on symbolic associations of nakedness seems to take us beyond arbitrary social conventions to something with a capacity for much more universal recognition and understanding.

A full survey of biblical material on nakedness and laying bare would be a much larger task than can be accomplished here. But we have already said enough to imply that specific judgments about the meaning of bodily nakedness need to be placed in context within their social framework in order for us to understand them. It is also worth adding that many of the full range of associations with nakedness mentioned above—destitution, vulnerability, and so on—appear to be 'in play.' If the word *'erwâ* (naked) is used in Leviticus purely with a sexual connotation,[8] it does not follow that this is the *only* kind of meaning it, or associated words such as 'make naked,' may be given.

Nakedness in the Beginning

The most obvious discussion of nakedness in the Old Testament, one related to many of the subsequent references to both nakedness and clothing, is in the Genesis account of creation and fall in Genesis 2.4–3.24. We are told in Genesis 2.25 that the man and woman were 'naked, and not ashamed.' Later on, after eating of the tree of the knowledge of good and evil, from which they have been forbidden to eat, they realize their nakedness. They seek to cover themselves from

---

7   See also 2 Samuel 10.1–5.
8   Boyd V Seevers, *in* Willem A VanGemeren (ed), *New International Dictionary of Old Testament Theology and Exegesis* (Exeter: Paternoster, 1997) p 527f.

each other and hide themselves from God, until God (presumably as an act of mercy) offers them better clothing in the form of animal skins.

At least one commentator[9] suggests that the not-ashamed-nakedness of 2.25 is mentioned only to offer us a contrast with their being clothed later on. But this does not block off the obvious question: *should* the man and woman have felt shame initially at their nakedness? The suggestion behind the question asked by God—'Who told you that you were naked?'—appears to imply that their unselfconsciousness was not a failure or a problem. Their nakedness was not something God expected them naturally to be conscious of.

Stephen Lambden[10] notes a three-fold transition here: (1) an initial nakedness and unashamedness, (2) being clothed in fig-leaf aprons and (3) being clothed in 'coats of skins.' He states that primordial 'nakedness' and 'unashamedness' most probably indicates that human relationships were originally characterized by innocence and mutual trust and respect. Much traditional Christianity, because of this passage, has thought of the awareness of nakedness as a manifestation of guilt, expressed as shame; but this is not the meaning of the Hebrew words. What is conventionally translated as 'to be ashamed' often means rather 'have a sense of being let down' or 'be disappointed.'[11]

We may note, in any event, that there is no obvious evidence of any 'return' to unselfconscious nakedness in the vision of apocalyptic consummation in the book of Revelation. Rather, there are a number of suggestions of clothing, typically of pure, white linen robes. There is a very obvious allusion to the Genesis story in Revelation 3.18, when the Christians of Laodicea are encouraged to clothe themselves with white garments, that 'the shame of their nakedness' may not be revealed. In Revelation 19.8 we see the Bride of Christ clothed in 'fine linen, bright and clean.' Yet this clothing turns out to have a special character; it is 'the righteous acts of the saints.'

It seems, then, that the shame and the nakedness, and the clothing which covers or takes away shame (covering and taking away are not quite the same thing, of course), serve a special function here. In this context, they symbolize the state of the unrighteous before God, and of the effect of the deeds done by the saints. Where Paul can speak of the results of our lives in terms of the purification of precious metal which will survive a refining fire (1 Corinthians 3.12–15), John can speak of the deeds of the saints as a process of clothing of the church in a bright wedding garment. That Christians may be exhorted to be 'put on [that is, 'be clothed with'] the Lord Jesus Christ' (Romans 13.14) implies a similar response to the phenomenon of spiritual nakedness. There are in fact a number of references in the epistles to this kind of 'putting on.' We see this in the context of a discussion of resurrection life (1 Corinthians 15.53, 54; 2 Corinthians 5.2, 3), baptism (Galatians 3.27, perhaps Colossians 3.10), and the explicit contrast in Ephesians 4.22–24, which

9   S R Driver, *Westminster Commentaries: Genesis* (London: Methuen, 1948) p 43.
10   Stephen N Lambden in Paul Morris and Deborah Sawyer (ed), *A Walk in the Garden* (Sheffield: JSOT Press, 1992) p 74.
11   James Barr, *The Garden of Eden and the Hope of Immortality* (London: SCM Press, 1992) p 63.

some English translations make obvious (RSV 'put off' 4.22, 'put on' 4.24).

We see from this that nakedness is used powerfully in symbolic association with issues of sin and guilt, and clothing (of a very particular sort!) serves as a remedy for this nakedness. Yet just as this nakedness is not necessarily the unclothedness of the body, so the clothing is not a physical covering (a better replacement for fig leaves, animal skins or the latest form of breathable water-proof jacket). Jesus takes the need for clothing for granted, but appears to do so in parallel with the need for food; these are necessary matters, which God cares about, because he cares for his creation (Matthew 6.24–34). Nakedness may provide an occasion for sexual temptation (2 Samuel 11.2), and sexual impurity is taken very seriously. But the symbolic language of nakedness is not restricted to matters of sexual sin and guilt. Instead it seems designed to threaten exposure of a much wider range of sins, all of them things we would prefer to be hidden.

5

Nakedness and the Body in Christian Tradition

New Testament Period Judaism and the Early Church

During the intertestamental and New Testament periods, many Jewish leaders were bitterly opposed to the attempted Hellenization of their country. The introduction of the Greek gymnasium,[12] where men exercised naked, led Hellenistic Jews to wish to conceal their circumcision (and thereby their Jewishness).[13] This is a quite specific issue in a particular context. We find in the Book of Jubilees 3.31 the comment: 'On this account, it is prescribed on the heavenly tablets as touching all those who know the judgment of the law, that they should cover their shame, and not uncover themselves as the Gentiles uncover themselves.'[14] This is a strong condemnation of the Gentile nudity that accompanied Greek athletics. Jews who took part in Greek athletics (1 Maccabees 1.10–15) may have argued, though, that as a matter of principle, in view of Adam's initial nakedness, their nudity was nothing untoward.

The earliest writings of the Christian church show little evidence of the negative attitude towards sexuality and nudity that so characterize later years. Negative attitudes grew slowly among some segments of the faith, and were by no means universal. The writings of early Christians such as Irenaeus and Tertullian make it clear that they had no ethical reservations about communal nudity. Chris-

---

12 The Greek word for naked is *gymnos*, which naturally forms part of the etymological root of *gymnasium*.
13 Frank Bottomley, *Attitudes to the Body in Western Christendom* (London: Lepus Books, 1979) p 25.
14 Translation in R H Charles, *Apocrypha and Pseudepigrapha of the Old Testament* (Oxford: Clarendon Press, 1913).

tian historian Roy Bowen Ward notes that 'Christian morality did not originally preclude nudity...There is a tendency to read history backward and assume that early Christians thought the same way mainstream Christians do today. We attribute the present to the past.'[15]

For the first several centuries of Christianity, it was the custom to baptize men, women and children together nude. This ritual played a very significant role in the early church. The accounts are numerous and detailed. Margaret Miles notes that 'naked baptism was observed as one of the two essential elements in Christian initiation, along with the invocation of the Trinity...In the fourth century instructions for baptism throughout the Roman Empire stipulated naked baptism without suggestion of innovation or change from earlier practices.'[16]

A typical historical account comes from Cyril of Jerusalem, bishop of Jerusalem from AD 387 to 417: 'As soon, then, as ye entered, ye put off your tunic... Having stripped yourselves, ye were naked; in this also imitating Christ, who was stripped naked on the Cross, and by his nakedness *put off from himself the principalities and powers, and openly triumphed over them on the tree.*' After baptism, and clothed in white albs, St Cyril can say of the newly baptized 'O wondrous thing! ye were naked in the sight of all, and were not ashamed; for truly ye bore the likeness of the first-formed Adam, who was naked in the garden, and was not ashamed.'[17] Cyril is explicit, however, in conceiving of the act of unclothing as an 'image of putting off the old man with his deeds' (Colossians 3.9), which may make us wonder whether the 'wondrous thing' is the willingness to repent rather than the lack of blushing at one's physical nudity. J C Cunningham notes in any event that 'There is nothing in the present rubrics of the Roman rite against doing this today. In fact, in the Eastern rites the rubrics even state the option of nude adult baptism.'[18]

The negative attitude to physical nakedness grew out of a mixture of Christianity and a legalistic tendency within traditional Judaism. Lambden writes that '...Jews did not generally share with their Hellenistic neighbours the notion of the natural beauty of the naked human body.'[19] For many others, the negative attitude grew out of pre-existing personal and cultural prejudices. Clement of Alexandria, in the late 2nd century, and Cyprian, in the mid 3rd century, both condemned the nudity common in Roman public baths, primarily because it offended their personal ideas of female modesty. Jerome, in the late 4th and the early 5th centuries, also condemned nude bathing, especially for women. It is notable that he is also concerned to condemn a fixation on clothing and fashion![20]

15 Roy Bowen Ward, 'Women in Roman Baths,' *Harvard Theological Review* 85.2, 1992, pp 125–147.
16 Margaret R Miles, *Carnal Knowing: Female Nakedness and Religious Meaning in the Christian West* (Boston: Beacon, 1989) p 33.
17 Cyril of Jerusalem, Lecture XX (Second Lecture on the Mysteries) 2, *in* P Schaff and H Wace (eds), *Nicene and Post-Nicene Fathers*, Second Series, Volume VII (Edinburgh: T&T Clark, 1989 reprint) p 147.
18 J C Cunningham, 'De Nuditate Habituque,' *Nude and Natural* 11.1, 1991, pp 47–51.
19 Stephen N Lambden *in* Paul Morris and Deborah Sawyer, *A Walk in the Garden* (Sheffield: JSOT Press, 1992) p 83.
20 Jerome, *Letter XXII, in* P Schaff and H Wace, *Nicene and Post-Nicene Fathers*, Second Series, Volume VI (Edinburgh: T&T Clark, 1989 reprint) p 36, §32, p 194, p 218.

On the other hand, in the same period, Jovinian, a Christian monk, campaigned actively in favour of public baths. In 4th century Antioch, as in many late classical cities, nudity had remained a fact of life. Nudity and sexual shame were questions of social status; the way people felt about being naked, or seeing others naked, depended to a large extent on their social situation.[21] At the top of society, nudity in public baths expressed the ease of the well-to-do, moving without trace of sexual shame in front of their inferiors. 'An Antiochene lady would strip down in front of her mixed retinue.' However, 'The sexual vulnerability of poor girls was simply part of their general passivity to the powerful.'

Peter Brown documents in the preaching of John Chysostom the contrasting teaching that all human beings were equal. He writes:

As Christianity gained more power in late Roman society, the sense that all human beings were equal, because levelled into a sombre democracy of sexual shame, made itself felt throughout the Mediterranean...Christian men and women were urged...to extend the heightened awareness of their own bodies so as to embrace with compassion the bodies of others. They must learn to see the faceless poor as sharing bodies like their own—bodies at risk, bodies gnawed by the bite of famine, disease and destitution, and subtly ravaged by the common catastrophe of lust.[22]

Augustine and After

In marked contrast to most Greek and Syrian writers, Augustine became influential in identifying the moment in Genesis 3.7 with an instant of clearly felt sexual shame. Brown comments:

As soon as they had made their own wills independent of the will of God, parts of Adam and Eve became resistant to their own conscious will. Their bodies were touched with a disturbing new sense of the alien, in the form of sexual sensations that escaped their control. A tiny but ominous symptom— in Adam's case, the stirring of an erection over which he had no control— warned them both of the final slipping of the body as whole from the soul's familiar embrace at death.[23]

Christian preachers exhibit a movement towards the emphasis of a common humanity in the reality of bodily vulnerability both to decay and control by alien, ungodly lusts and aspirations. God had created the human body with a purpose; Adam had violated this and brought upon it the double shame of death and lust.

The new sensibility to the body and to nudity demonstrates a change in the collective imagination of the ancient world.[24] Late Roman codes of upper-class

---

21 Peter Brown, *The Body and Society* (London: Faber and Faber, 1988) p 315f.
22 Peter Brown, *op cit*, pp 316, 317.
23 Peter Brown, *op cit*, p 417, citing as authorities Augustine, *de civitate Dei* 14.23, 25 and *de Genesi ad litteram* 9.9.17.
24 Peter Brown, *op cit*, p 437.

dress made the social status of their wearers more blatant than ever before. In doing so, they carefully sheathed the body itself. Emperors no longer showed their power by posing in the nude, thereby recapturing the heroic ease and readiness associated with the deathless gods. High born or low, emperor or beggar, all were formed from the self-same stuff. 'The poor wretch whom we despise, whom we cannot so much as look at, and the very sight of whom turns our stomachs, is human like ourselves, is made of the same clay as we are, is formed out of the same elements. All that he suffers we too may suffer.'[25] 'Whether we wear silk or rags we are all at the mercy of the same desire. It does not fear the royal purple; it does not disdain the squalor of the mendicant.'[26]

Some Christians continued, though, to use nudity as a symbol of renouncing the world to follow Christ. Margaret Miles writes: 'in the thirteenth century, Saint Bernard of Clairvaux popularized the idea of nudity as symbolic imitation of Christ; it took Saint Francis to act out this metaphor. Francis announced his betrothal to Lady Poverty by publicly stripping off his clothing and flinging it at the feet of his protesting father and the local bishop.'[27] Several Christian sects have practised nudity as part of their faith, including the German Brethren of the Free Spirit, in the 13th century, the Picards, in 15th century France, and, most famously, the Adamites, in the early 15th century in the Netherlands.

The Renaissance

The renaissance brought about a new distinction between the naked and the nude. To be naked was simply to be oneself, without disguise, vulnerably human. To be nude is to be seen as a naked object, a thing displayed. Medieval moral theology distinguished four symbolic meanings of nudity, reminiscent of some of our categories in the discussion in chapter 3 above, as follows:

- *Nuditus naturalis*—the natural state of humanity, conducive to humanity, like the words from the Ash Wednesday liturgy 'Remember you are dust and to dust you shall return.' This kind of nudity occurs in representations of paradise, the last judgment, the resurrection.
- *Nuditus temporalis*—lack of earthly goods due to poverty or voluntary abnegation, as in the case of apostles, ascetics and members of religious orders.
- *Nuditus virtualis*—the symbol of innocence, the soul denuded of its rags of guilt, the divesting of outward appearances. Often related to the sacrament of confession.
- *Nuditus criminalis*—a sign of lust, bestiality, vanity and the absence of all virtues. This form of nudity explains the naked representation of pagan divinities, devils and sinful humans.[28]

25   Jerome, *Letter LXXVII.6*, in P Schaff and H Wace (eds), *Nicene and Post-Nicene Fathers,* Second Series, Volume VI (Edinburgh: T&T Clark, 1989 reprint) p 160.
26   Jerome, *Letter LXXIX.10*, in P Schaff and H Wace (eds), *op cit,* p 167. See Peter Brown, *The Body and Society* (London: Faber and Faber, 1989) p 317.
27   Margaret R Miles, *Carnal Knowing: Female Nakedness and Religious Meaning in the Christian West* (Boston: Beacon, 1989) p xii.
28   Frank Bottomley, *Attitudes to the Body in Western Christendom* (London: Lepus Books, 1979) p 180.

A connection can be seen between these and the significance of Old Testament nakedness. Each of these has had an influence on how we view nakedness today. Instead of separating them, though, we appear to have blurred the boundaries, linking the first with the fourth and so on.

Nudity was fairly common in medieval and renaissance society, especially in the public baths and within the family setting. Lawrence Wright observes that 'The communal tub had…one good reason; the good reason was the physical difficulty of providing hot water. The whole family and their guests would bathe together while the water was hot…Ideas of propriety were different from ours, the whole household and the guests shared the one and only sleeping apartment and wore no night clothes until the sixteenth century. It was not necessarily rude to be nude.'[29]

The high-ranking nobles of Edward IV's court were permitted by law to display their naked genitals below a short tunic, and contemporary reports indicate that they did so. Chaucer commented on the use of this fashion in *The Parson's Tale,* written in the late 13th Century. He complains that some men's garments, were so short 'that thurgh hire shortnesse ne covere nat the shameful membres of man, to wikked entente.'[30]

Between the 14th and mid-17th centuries, and especially during the reign of Louis XIV, women would often leave their bodices loose and open or even entirely undone, exposing the nipple or even the whole of the breast, a practice confirmed by numerous historical accounts. The Venetian ambassador, writing in 1617, described Queen Anne of Denmark as wearing a dress which displayed her bosom 'bare down to the pit of the stomach.' In 1445 Guillaume Jouvenal des Ursins became Chancellor of France and his brother, an ecclesiastic, wrote to him urging him to tell the king that he should not allow the ladies of his household to wear gowns with front openings that revealed their breast and nipples.[31]

The 'naturalness' of art-forms which involve the naked body, both in their production and critical assessment, is a product of trajectories in culture. The inheritance of the 19th and 20th centuries in Western Europe have created in today's society a semi-hiddenness which promotes the naked body in the guise of pornography, or the objectification of the form or appearance of the naked body.

There are some who would defend this objectification, and only complain of any exploitation in its production. As long as those who are (say) photographed give their free consent, there is nothing wrong. It is against such attitudes and defences, as much as against those attitudes which demean or hate the body and its exposure, that naturists seek to present their own views.

---

29   Lawrence Wright, *Clean and Decent: The Fascinating History of the Bathroom and Water Closet* (London: University of Toronto Press, 1960) p 23.

30   (Ed John H Fisher), *The Complete Poetry and Prose of Geoffrey Chaucer* (New York: Holt, Rinehart and Winston, 1977) p 364 (Parson's Tale, at line 422).

31   Aileen Ribeiro, *Dress and Morality* (London: Batsford, 1986) p 52, and note 26 on p 175.

6
Naturism, Nakedness and the Body

Naturists are not entirely agreed amongst themselves about the meaning of naturism, or the significance of nakedness. This disagreement shows itself in a variety of ways. We could hope to express this in shorthand as a contrast between those who see naturism as a whole way of life (where nakedness has an important role) and those who see delight in nakedness as the sole characteristic of naturism. But that would be a bit too swift. In this chapter we give an abstract presentation, which we will need to relate to actual naturism later on.

Naturism as Lifestyle

It is true that there are people who accept the label 'naturist' and who regard their beliefs as constituting a whole 'way of life.' It is a way of life in which shame and fear of nakedness have no part, but also one in which clothing has a clear function (for protecting against cold, to give just one obvious example). These naturist beliefs might form part of a philosophy of life in which other commitments, for example to environmentally friendly food production, or to the importance of family relationships and to trust and honesty within them, will all have their part.

In this sense naturism can be (will be) much more than just a hobby. A naturist who holds nakedness as just one part of a commitment to a perceived naturalness of lifestyle and attitude towards neighbours and the world may find it very hard indeed to separate out bodily nakedness as a defining part of this philosophy of life. What to an outsider might seem to be most distinctive about such a person—that he or she does not wear clothes for much of the time—can look like the defining element of the naturist's 'naturism.' To the naturist, it may be much harder to distinguish the various elements. The naturist might actually see the judgment that 'nakedness is what matters most' as a sign of distorted and fragmented thinking on the part of the non-naturist. The non-naturist sees nudity as almost pornographic, where the naturist sees it as an integrated element of a natural lifestyle.

To a naturist of this sort, it matters a lot that questions of body image are of relatively minor importance. Admittedly, where there is also a concern with good health, as there is likely to be to some extent, the issue of being under- or overweight might be a matter of concern; but body image then takes on an instrumental importance in relation to healthy living. The really important thing is that people be accepted as they are; their acceptability does not depend on their fitting some ideal of body image set by arbitrary cultural ideals of youth, shape and fitness.

Naturism as Nakedness

Now, compare this with forms of naturism which celebrate nakedness as an expression of the capacity of the human body to conform to certain ideal standards of bodily beauty. This form of naturism may contain some self-conscious attempt to adhere to standards of idealized bodily beauty (symmetry, for example), perhaps inherited from the classical world, notably from aspects of ancient Greek culture.

Prima facie, this second version of naturism looks likely to exclude much of humanity from its ranks, and certainly it could do so. 'Only the young and beautiful [by the standards of youth and beauty currently in fashion!] need apply.' Nakedness (for those who conform to the right body shape) is to be promoted; clothing, at least regarding its relevance to this form of naturism, may be a sign of failure and shame. It would be possible, however, for this form of naturism to develop its own more far-reaching 'life programme.' Just about anyone could participate; there might be regimes of exercise, hygiene and body grooming which all ages and shapes can at least participate in with a view to trying to come as near as each individual can do to the perceived image of bodily perfection. (There will also need to be a decision by naturists of this kind whether the body images they worship are to be naturally achieved, or whether they are pure ends detached from means, so that cosmetic surgery and the like may make their contribution.)[32]

Conflicting Ideals?

If these two images of naturism are anything like accurate portrayals of the forms which naturism may actually take—and some recent media attention has included examples of each, implying some rivalry between them—we will have at least two very different sets of attitudes to respond to. It is worth adding that for neither set of attitudes does nakedness in itself seem to be such a dramatically significant aspect of the package that it suggests we can evaluate it purely and simply in terms of not-wearing-clothes. A culture of open acceptance, without prejudging people according to body shape, possessions, skin colour, nationality or sex, is something which Christians are clearly likely to express a very distinct and positive interest in. Thus, we will need to address the question whether, from a Christian perspective, naturism at least conceived in this sort of way could make a positive contribution to human life.

So much, for the moment, for the first form of naturism. As to the 'ideal image' form: apart from the particular feature of public nakedness, one could argue that a great deal of contemporary life is consistent with this attitude in any event.

---

32 It is tempting to contrast these two forms under two separate terms or labels, and to see them as historically separate, but it seems that they are not as separate in practice as might be expected. The label 'gymnosophy' was used for some naturists earlier this century, borrowed from a Greek word used originally to characterize a 'Hindu' sect in the time of Alexander the Great. Certainly, this word implies something like a 'way of life,' and in practice was used for something more like our second form of naturism. However, the words naturism, nudism and gymnosophy have been used with sufficient interchangeability in recent history that it is probably best to avoid confusion which could be caused by marking the distinction in this way.

Clothing, cosmetics, exercise, diets, surgery and a whole host of advertising and advice seek to reinforce a relatively narrow range of ideal images. Whereas in its naturist forms the ideal might be sustained by a sort of religious vision, in everyday life it is often the shareholders of cosmetics companies, clothing stores, and others who have a vested interest in at least sustaining the vision, whatever particular form it takes.

The religious vision of the naturist may imply something about self-fulfilment and even imply that one owes it to one's fellow humanity to be as 'beautiful' as possible. The language of *self*-fulfilment is often present or at least implied in advertising for clothing and food products, but who else one owes a 'duty of beauty' to (to invent a phrase for the purpose!) is usually more restricted, though not absolutely so. To be naked before one's husband or wife is not to experience any appropriate *real* shame, as one would about sin. The shame is rather in not looking like Gwyneth Paltrow (or Juliette Binoche, or…) or like Leonardo diCaprio (or Sylvester Stallone or…)

Sex, Eroticism and Nakedness

In neither of the accounts of naturism offered did we need to give any special place to a discussion of the sexual connotations of nakedness. It might be thought that concern with an ideal body image *must* have sexual implications. It seems clear enough, after all, that the way in which idealized naked and semi-naked bodies are used in the marketing of products works on an association of the naked body with the satisfaction of sexual desire. Presumably a link is forged thereby to other forms of desire-satisfaction more immediately relevant to the product.

However, the connection of nakedness and sex, though it may *seem* inescapable, need not necessarily be so. We do not need to refer back to our list of associations with nakedness earlier in the booklet to see the truth of this. A community of naturist ascetics dedicated to the cultivation of an ideal body through lives of celibacy and self-denial is, after all, entirely believable. If the question occurs to anyone 'What would the point of it be?' we could easily enough invent a plausible-sounding answer—for instance, the cultivation of the image of a physically-conceived deity, as an act of homage. Just as relevant, and more significant for contemporary life, would be a perfectly reasonable counter-question from any such naturist ascetic. He or she could ask what the point of *our* culture's obsession with sexual activity, or other forms of superficial desire satisfaction, might be.

The two different accounts or forms of naturism are, of course, idealizations. Both have a grounding in reality, though the beliefs and practices of individuals or groups of naturists may not conform precisely to either. But they will serve to provide a useful framework for our discussion of the *Christian* significance of naturism.

7
Practice and Experience

In the first form we have sketched, naturism is a way of living in harmony with nature. It engenders respect for oneself, for others and for the environment in which we live and move, and is very much a family activity. The Naturist Foundation states as one of its aims: 'We believe that the family is the basis of all society and that naturist sunbathing should be regarded as a family occupation.'[33]

Maurice Parmelee made a study of the benefits of naturism in the 1930s. In his book *Nudism in Modern Life* he said that: 'The habit of wearing clothes makes the skin anaemic and hinders the vaso-motor reflexes, thus disturbing the circulation of the blood and rendering the skin abnormally sensitive to heat and cold.'[34]

So it has been claimed that there is something healthy about going without clothes! Naturist activity appears to be able to satisfy both mental and physical health and both must be nourished and satisfied. Physically, time spent naked is said to build up a resistance to cold. The contact of fresh air with skin is beneficial and many naturist doctors would prescribe fresh air as an aid to recovery.

All this is far removed from the sexual connotations we generally give to nudity. Christians within the naturist movement discover in all this a freedom that complements their Christian faith. One writes:

> The moral climate in a sun club is unmatched anywhere else. Parents can allow their children to wander undressed throughout the grounds without a worry as to their moral and physical safety. Car doors are left unlocked, purses and wallets lie unattended beside vacant sun beds. Idyllic? In a way, yes. Escapist? Probably, but it is only a very unusual breed of person who does not need to switch off occasionally from the stresses of life. Perfect? No, we are all only human, with all the frailties of humanity. We are not in naturism to create the perfect society, simply to enjoy some of what is good and beautiful in the life God has given us for our pleasure.

Naturism is clearly very different from the nudity portrayed in magazines, newspapers, video and television. It is not for titillation. Mass nudity is far from erotic. Uncovered genitalia do not lead to an inability to control sexual urges. Nor does clothing prevent rape or assault, or hinder amorous advances.

The realism of social nudity, or naturism, is rather a let-down sexually speaking. As a naturist once described,

> There are no orgies, men have no trouble keeping their penises under control, women don't have to fight off hoards of assailants...Boring isn't it? But what

---

33 *Naturism 2000* (Orpington: Naturism Foundation, 1993) p 3. (The Naturist Federation is a Naturist Club in North Kent, and is affiliated to the CCBN.)
34 Maurice Parmelee, *Nudism in Modern Life: the young gymnosophy* (London: J Lane, 1933) p 109.

you find is a greater sense of freedom, more willingness to converse, more willingness too to help those in trouble and a greater sense of fun.

Must nude be crude? No; life in a naturist club, or a naturist resort, is just about doing things which one generally does with clothes on, but unclothed when the circumstances permit it. If it is cold or pouring with rain one puts clothes on. It is nothing weird, but purely natural. It means not just lying in the sun but joining in sports and recreational activities, swimming, badminton, miniten (a naturist version of tennis), petanque, barbecues, picnics—the list is endless—and it also creates a large social network.

One of the most common recreational activities for all naturists is swimming. Modern bathing costumes have become smaller and smaller in recent years and naturists prefer to experience the joy of plunging through the water unhampered rather than deal with a soggy bathing costume. On beaches during the summer, one sees hordes of ordinary people almost, but not quite, naked. The 'private parts' remain covered because they are regarded as in some way shameful and so destined always to be hidden. The reasons for this attitude towards these particular parts, all the functions of which are essential to human life and in no way contrary to our nature, ought at least to be questioned.

Clubs take links between nakedness and pornography very seriously. All have strict guidelines on such matters as admission for membership, who they allow to visit and photography. It is true that the respectable public face of a naturist club could be abused by a group desiring to focus on sexual promiscuity, and the CCBN is very much aware of the dangers both of misperception of their own activities and abuse of them by others.

Christian Naturists?

Many naturists belong to local churches and regularly worship God; obviously such people see no conflict between Christian morality and regular social nudity. One of the authors, growing up in a family where naturism and Christianity have both been major influences, and writing as one whose parents are very involved in the naturist movement, has discovered that many naturists have no problem being open about their Christianity with other naturists. However, they cannot be as open about their naturism with other Christians without experiencing or fearing hostility and ostracism.

Naturists present a kind of acceptance of their bodies not much in evidence in today's society, but something which is compatible with the Christian faith. A Christian naturist writes, 'God certainly asks us to accept ourselves and our bodies as he made them. He must wonder at the sense of guilt in his creation turning good into bad, a source of joy into a source of misery.' Another remarks: 'It certainly isn't naturism that I find incompatible with Christianity, but shame about our bodies to me sits uneasy with knowing the God whose creation is good beyond measure. God gave us our bodies to live in and to enjoy. He gave us our sexuality too to take delight in. He gave us our intelligence so that we might know how to enjoy and not to abuse both.'

8
So is Naturism Acceptable?

Our society's nudity taboo applies to specific areas of the body only. Practically this means that for both sexes sight of the region extending from the waist to the upper thighs is forbidden while for females the prohibition extends also to the chest area. The various reasons for the taboo, that the genitals may become aroused, to maintain values of virginity, chastity and purity, and the connection between these parts of the body and eliminatory functions which are dealt with in private, are understandable. Yet, as Francis Bennion writes, this may give rise to damaging consequences: 'to prohibit exposure of a particular area of the human anatomy leads to that area becoming the subject of unwholesome, even unhealthy curiosity. For some this curiosity may become obsessive, or in rare cases pathological.'[35]

In his book *Bodies of knowledge*, which looks at the psychological significance of the nude in art, Liam Hudson speaks of the contradictory responses that the body demands of us because it has an excretory function as well as a reproductive one. The anthropologist Mary Douglas writes: 'The symbolic lives of both primitive and more sophisticated societies are organized to a remarkable degree around the oppositions of purity and dirt.'[36] The body then is inherently 'dangerous,' as we run the risk of confusion in the simultaneous and contradictory presence of desire and disgust.

Opposition to human nakedness seems to have reached its height towards the end of the 19th century. The late Victorians were particularly censorious about male nudity, as when boys and men were innocently bathing in a public place, and various bans were enforced. Attitudes in the Victorian period were not uniform, of course, as a reading of the celebrated diaries of the Anglican clergyman Francis Kilvert, and his resentment of cumbersome swimwear, make plain![37]

Nudity and Sex
The Longford Committee on Pornography said flatly that sex is essentially a private affair. Even if they were right, does this justify a ban on simple nudity when divorced from sexual activity or arousal?

Nakedness cannot automatically be associated with lust. It is not reasonable to cover food in the marketplace just because someone might be tempted by gluttony. It is not reasonable to ban nudity, simply because an individual might be tempted to lust. Appreciation for the beauty of a member of the other sex, nude or otherwise, cannot be equated automatically with lust. Pope John Paul II writes:

---

35 Francis Bennion, *The Sex Code. Morals for Moderns* (London: Weidenfeld and Nicolson, 1992) p 52.
36 Quoted in Liam Hudson, *Bodies of Knowledge. The Psychological Significance of the Nude in Art* (London: Weidenfeld and Nicolson, 1982) p 9.
37 Francis Kilvert (ed William Plomer), *Kilvert's Diary 1870-1879* (Harmondsworth: Penguin, 1977) 13 July 1875; 24 July 1873; 12 June 1874.

There are circumstances in which nakedness is not immodest. If someone takes advantage of such an occasion to treat the person as an object of enjoyment (even if his action is purely internal) it is only he who is guilty of shamelessness, not the other…Sexual modesty cannot then in any simple way be identified with the use of clothing, nor shamelessness with the absence of clothing and total or partial nakedness…Immodesty is present only when nakedness plays a negative role with regard to the value of the person, when its aim is to arouse concupiscence, as a result of which the person is put in the position of an object for enjoyment…There are certain objective situations in which even total nudity of the body is not immodest.[38]

Pornographic literature may contain correct statements concerning erotic and sexual processes. Yet in it truth is integrated into a perverse system of values and becomes lies. Helmut Thielicke writes that pornography falsifies the place of sex in humanity. It depersonalizes, biologizes and psychologizes it. The pornographer in his own person has missed the real meaning of the truth and its purpose, so that the 'untruth of the person makes the statement to be untrue.'[39]

Naturism appears as the total opposite of pornography. An article in the French Naturist Federation magazine on *Naturism and Sexuality* states that naturism, due to the mutual showing of the sex organs, represents the presence of sexuality in all naked activity, giving a sense of re-unification of humanity and a re-integration in personal and group relationships. Pornography proposes the opposite. It centres everything on the sex organs and contains elements of both obsession and of exhibitionism. In pornography the body is carved up and we are presented only with bodily parts, instead of the bodily integration that naturism seeks to provide, with the sexual taking its place within the integral nature of the whole person.[40]

The naturist movement has also always had to contend with the idea that nudism is what has been called 'a bizarre branch of neo-puritanism.' Either naturists are regarded as puritans or taken to be practising pornographers! Opponents veer from one extreme to the other. Naturists are as fond of clothing as most people provided that garments are used for their proper purpose, namely for warmth, adornment, hygiene and protection. It is *this* notion of propriety, and not one of horror of human nakedness, which informs their attitudes.

Dr G B Barker, consultant psychiatrist at a large London hospital, giving evidence to a 1969 Arts Council Working Party on the obscenity laws, said: 'I would state dogmatically that if nudity was accepted completely from the earliest age, there would be far less neurotic unhappiness, and less need for vicarious enjoyments of alternatives to sexuality (such as pornography). It is likely also that

---

38 John Paul II, *Love and Responsibility* (London: HarperCollins, 1981) quoting from the section 'The Metaphysics of Shame,' in order from: p 190, p 176, p 190, p 191.
39 Helmut Thielicke, *Theological Ethics I: Foundations* (London: A&C Black, 1968) p 552.
40 Marc-Alain Descamps, 'Naturism and Sexuality,' in *Naturism* (French Naturist Federation, 1992).

there would be less promiscuity, because promiscuity is based upon the neurotic inability to find or to form an adult relationship.'[41]

Naturism and Wholeness

Far from separating sex and putting it on one side, naturism integrates all human relationships. Women who are naturists have spoken of being ennobled and made equal. Very often the subjects of pornography and prostitution, naked women have become constrained to being sexual objects and playthings for men. Naturist women instead appear naked alongside men and children, and comment on the discretion which reigns in naturist centres. Treated as equals, they feel themselves infinitely more secure and at ease than on the streets of our cities.[42]

As well as mental health, there is also the positive joy in observing the beauty of the human form. It could be argued that beauty, freedom and naturalness are on one side of a coin, which on the reverse carries guilt, anxiety and neurosis. Yet to a significant degree perceptions of beauty and what is natural can be determined by arbitrary factors which imprison rather than set free. Mention of beauty can lead to those forms of naturism which stress the importance of certain body-images, and which work against some of the ideals we have mentioned, so that it is worth stressing the *appreciation* of the natural here, rather than the *imposition* of an arbitrary standard of beauty.

Nudity Taboos

Taboos obviously vary from society to society. What constitutes normality and conformity can only be decided when we consider the culture within which an individual is functioning. Even nudity taboos vary as to what parts of the body must be concealed. In some primitive tribes it is only the anal region that is private; in Saudi Arabia, for example, it includes the face.

The arbitrary nature of clothing is reflected too by different standards in different cultures. For example, a review of 190 world societies in 1951 found that, contrary to the standards of our own culture, relatively few considered exposure of a women's breast to be immodest. Julian Robinson observes:

...few cultural groups agree as to which parts of our bodies should be covered and which parts should be openly displayed...Indeed, many people find it difficult to comprehend the logic behind any other mode of clothing and adornment than what they are currently wearing, finding them all unnatural or even uncivilized. The thought of exposing or viewing those parts of the body which they generally keep covered so frightens or disgusts them that they call upon their lawmakers to protect them from such a possibility.[43]

---

41 Francis Bennion, *The Sex Code: Morals for Moderns* (London: Weidenfield and Nicolson, 1992) p 59.
42 Marc-Alain Descamps, 'Naturism and Sexuality,' in *Naturism* (French Naturist Federation, 1992).
43 Julian Robinson, *Body Packaging: A Guide to Human Sexual Display* (Los Angeles: Elysium Growth, 1988) p 36.

Kingsley Bond once wrote an article in the pictorial magazine *People* entitled *Topless Dresses and Morals*. He was an ex-missionary, and an Australian Methodist Minister. He wanted to know what was the difference between accepting brown-skinned people, bare in a warm climate, and the same with pink-skinned people in a warm climate. Having preached in churches at least half full of topless women, should he and others avert their gaze?[44]

Even in the same culture, taboos about what parts of the body could or could not be revealed have changed radically over time. Lois M Gurel writes: 'One must remember that clothing itself is neither moral or immoral. It is the breaking of traditions which makes it so.'[45]

9
Conclusion

We return now to our initial questions, and draw out some implications regarding the compatibility of naturism and Christianity. There appears, firstly, to be no biblical grounds either for a promotion of social nudity or for placing a complete ban on it. Clearly, though, there is an important distinction to be drawn between physical nakedness and sexual impurity. There is also the issue of concern for other people and for their own way of living.

Attitudes towards nakedness vary depending upon culture and historical era, as exemplified in the change in attitudes from the Victorian bathing machine era to the permissive attitudes of the 1960s. We can also see that again there has been a differentiation between nudity and sexual immorality. Naturist clubs continued to be created throughout the liberated sixties, but for the sake of a rather different nakedness than was being reflected elsewhere—promoting a traditional, simplistic, often archaic, unclothed lifestyle unchanged from the beginnings of naturism in the 1920s.

Christians who are not naturists often misunderstand this aspect of nakedness. In our churches, there is need for much education and openness to talk about issues of sexuality, to remove false taboos which we tend to have about our own bodies and to define the differences between what is impure and what is godly and properly natural to us. In this context, it is to be hoped that Christians who are naturists will be allowed to be honest about their views and given the

---

44 Quoted in Raymond L Grant, 'Should a Christian Join a Sun Club?' *Australian Sun and Health,* Spring 1992.
45 Lois M Gurel, *The Function of Dress: Dimensions of Dress and Adornment, a Book of Readings* (Duberque, IA: Hendell/Hunt, 1979) pp 3–7.

chance to explain how they understand nakedness from the Christian perspective. In turn, Christians who do not agree or who feel unable to participate may still respect their differing convictions.

Some naturists say that it is more fitting for a Christian than a non-Christian to be a naturist, given that Christians are new creations living before God, who need not know that shame which gives nakedness such symbolic potency. The form of naturism most compatible with Christianity lays more emphasis on naturalness than on nakedness. Naturists believe that the 'hang-up' about the body being shameful in itself, in whatever way, is both morally wrong and mentally harmful. This points to the fundamental difference of attitude between naturists, who are not frightened or ashamed of their bodies, and that of much of the world, which would seem to be so. In naturism one realizes that there are no truly private parts; all parts of the body serve their proper and honourable purpose and in this respect we are all alike.

We conclude from this review of the different aspects of nakedness that there is no essential conflict between Christianity and naturism, that there is nothing inherently sinful about the naked body, and that the realization of this is part of what it means to be at ease with oneself, to be healed, to be made whole.

There are, of course, caveats. Nakedness is not an end or a good in itself, and should not be forced upon anyone. Connected with this, Christian naturists might well be very circumspect about the promotion of public nudity if it would be likely to cause offence or discomfort for their fellow Christians, or just as (or even more) importantly for those who might be less inclined to listen to the Christian gospel because of their activities.

This negative note, though, should not obscure the importance of realizing the truth of the created goodness of our bodies, and their connection with the full reality of our salvation. C S Lewis writes of people being without clothes in his book *The Great Divorce*. He describes an 'imaginative supposal' of heaven in this way:

Long after that I saw people coming to meet us...some were naked, some robed. But the naked ones did not seem less adorned, and the robes did not disguise in those who wore them the massive grandeur of muscle and the radiant smoothness of flesh.[46]

One Christian naturist writes: 'Naturism isn't a panacea for the world's problems, but maybe the attitude of mind that allows you to accept the gift of your body as completely acceptable and as intended by the Giver is just one more step along the path towards a saner society.'

---

46   C S Lewis, *The Great Divorce* (Glasgow: Collins, 1946) p 29.